THE SANTASAURUS REX by

First published in 2023

This edition published in 2023

****

The Santasaurus

Ho Ho Ho! Merry Christmas!,

The magic of Christmas is nearly upon us, and Mrs Saurus and I have been busy here at the North Pole, making sure that everything is ready for the most wonderful time of the year. The Compi elves have been working hard preparing all the toys and making sure that this Christmas is extra special for you and all the other boys and girls around the world.

My Raptors are excited to pull my sleigh so that I can deliver all the presents. I hope you've been good this year.

I'm off to go and find my sleigh and the presents and make sure that everything is ready for Christmas Eve.

I hope you have a Roarsome Christmas and a Happy New Year, oh and I hope that you enjoy my story too.

Merry Christmas!,

"Twas the night before Christmas and all through the jungle, there was a terrible noise... an almighty rumble!"

Chapter One

No one quite knows how there came to be a jungle at the North Pole. It's not the first place that comes to mind when you think of a jungle, but to the dinosaurs that live there, it's widely accepted that it's magic, more specifically, the magic of Christmas that keeps it alive.

In most jungles, there are huge soaring tree canopies with wild and tangled branches that spread out across the treetops like an enormous patchy green blanket. This jungle is no different. On a sunny day, beams of sunlight can be seen shining through the tree-top canopy to the dense vegetation below, but unlike most jungles, this one has a sprinkling of fresh white snow that glistens all year round which makes it a truly magical place.

In the centre of the jungle is the village of Snøsted, this is where the dinosaurs live. Snøsted, like most towns, has many buildings which are used by its inhabitants. There are houses, shops, barns, stables and all the other things you would expect to find in any village. The most important building in the whole of the North Pole is the Workshop. This is the largest building of them all and it sits at the centre of Snøsted. From above the village looks like a shining star with the Workshop at its centre and the countless roads and streets leading away like beams of light. The dinosaurs' homes are decorated like Christmas gingerbread houses and each one is painted in different festive colours. There are reds, greens, blues and gold. Everywhere you look there are trees, they surround the village and are on every street. Each one is covered in snow and decorated with twinkling fairy lights.

In the middle of the town square in front of the Workshop, is the tallest Norway Spruce Christmas tree you've ever seen. This tree is decorated with huge colourful baubles and ornaments that hang from every branch. There are also what seems like miles of tinsel and beautiful bright twinkling lights that run from the bottom to the top of the tree wrapping around and around its many branches. Right at the very top, there sits a giant silver star that shines as bright as any star in the night sky, maybe even brighter. Snøsted is a beautiful and busy place, it's always bustling with activity especially at this time of year with everyone working together for Christmas. Despite the freezing temperatures outside, the warmth and love in Snøsted can be felt by all. The magic of Christmas truly lives in this jungle at the North Pole.

Chapter Two

The North Pole Jungle is home to many dinosaurs. All shapes, sizes and species but the most famous of them all is the Santasaurus Rex. The Santasaurus Rex is a Tyrannosaurus Rex but unlike most Tyrannosaurus Rex he's not a huge scary dinosaur that's always trying to terrify and eat everyone. No, he's the biggest, kindest dinosaur that you ever could meet. Everyone at the North Pole knows him and he knows everyone at the North Pole, in fact, he knows everyone everywhere. The Santasaurus not only knows everyone at the North Pole, but he knows them by name, and he will always say hello and take time to talk to people when he sees them. Each year on Christmas Eve the Santasaurus Rex sets out on his sleigh to deliver presents to children all around the world.

The Santasaurus is excitedly getting ready for another

busy Christmas Eve. "This is my favourite time of year," he thought to himself. "All year we are busy with the preparation for this one night, the night where I get to fly around the world and deliver all the gifts and spread festive cheer, happiness and joy," he continued. "I've checked my list twice as you can never be too careful. I don't want to get anything wrong. This year is going to be as special as ever, if not, even more special," he said to himself joyfully. There was no reason why this year should be any more special than any other, he just really loved what he did. Mrs. Saurus, in her wisdom, had written him a list so he didn't forget anything.

Mrs Saurus is married to the Santasaurus. They have been married for longer than anyone can remember and for more years than she cares to think about. She can often be seen in the shops and cafes of Snøsted, shopping and talking with the locals. She is a warm, nurturing, kind-hearted dinosaur. She is always dressed festively and impeccably in her cosy red dress with its white fur trim, black shoes, white gloves and red-rimmed glasses. More often than not she will have on her crisp white waist-length apron over her dress which has a leather strap which goes around the neck and another that ties around her waist. On the front is a small pocket with a Christmas tree embroidered on it. Mrs Saurus loves being in the Village but the thing she loves most, apart from Santasaurus, is assisting him in his preparations for Christmas Eve.

The Santasaurus is a jolly old dino but sometimes he can be a very forgetful jolly old dino. "Ok… where is my list?", he asked himself. "I know I have my list so that I don't forget anything, but I have forgotten where I put my list," he thought as he roamed from room to room looking in all the places he could think to look. He took his small wire-framed spectacles from his top pocket and placed them on and continued looking. He looked on the wooden table next to his favourite chair where he would sit and read in the evenings. The large chair was wonderfully comfortable, and he would often fall asleep in it. The table was piled high with books, all Christmas books, naturally. "No, it's not there, where could it be? … Oh, here it is," he said as he walked back into the kitchen. He had put it on the fridge door for safe keeping, held in place with a magnet in the shape of himself in his Santa Suit with the words 'Have a Roarsome Christmas' written underneath. Mrs. Saurus had made him the magnet many years ago and like him it was starting to look a little tired.

"Right, let's check the list," he said.

- Santa Suit

- Sleigh

- Sack full of presents

- Present list (make sure you check it twice!)

- ~~MORE MINCE PIES~~

He had added the words 'MORE MINCE PIES' to the bottom of the list but Mrs Saurus had crossed it out as apparently more mince pies are not essential. "I think more mince pies are very essential," he had argued, but Mrs Saurus had made it clear that he had enough to get on with without stuffing his face with mince pies.

He put his list in his pocket with the thought of hot mince pies dancing around his head which was making his tummy rumble. "Well, lots to do so I'd better get on," he said.

Chapter Three

The Santasaurus Rex has been busy trying to check everything on his list but so far, it's not been going well at all. "Oh dear, today is not going to plan and I'm running out of time," he said, his hands on his hips and a confused look on his face. He has so far spent the morning all a fluster as he can't find his sleigh. He's been crashing and bashing around but there is no sign of it anywhere. Not only is the sleigh missing but so are all the presents that he needs to deliver. He's looked high, he's looked low, and he's even looked in between but he cannot remember where he has left them. "Where have I left that sleigh?" he asked himself frustratedly, "and those presents?" He wasn't sure how you lose a sleigh that big and with that many presents on it, but somehow, he had. There really were an awful lot of presents too.

Each year the amount of Christmas letters delivered to

the North Pole was increasing and so were the amounts of presents. This year was no exception. The things that the children were asking for were vast and varied too. There were skateboards and scooters, dolls and computers, planes and trains, and everything in between. Someone had even asked for a wooden Rocking Horse in the shape of a motorbike. "I remember when the children on the Good list got sweets and fruit and the children that were unfortunate enough to find themselves on the Naughty list got a lump of coal," he thought as he started to daydream of years gone by. These days he had a lot to deliver, at least he was supposed to have a lot to deliver but he still could not remember where he had left his sleigh and the towering stack of presents.

Having no luck in his search he decided that he needed to make a better plan of what he could do. He went and sat in his favourite spot on an old blue wooden bench which sits outside his house where he lives with Mrs Saurus and started to think. He likes to sit there because from that spot he has a panoramic view of Snøsted, and he can see all the other houses and buildings with their decorations up and their Christmas lights on. After a little while a couple of ideas came to him. The first involved going to the kitchen and getting some mince pies but he decided that this idea wouldn't help much so he decided to go with his second idea. "I know what to do," he said. "If I'm going to find my lost sleigh and the presents then I need to retrace my steps and start today again and go back to the beginning." So, he made his way back to where he started every day. His bedroom.

Chapter Four

Standing in the middle of his bedroom, he looked around and thought about what he had done when he first woke up and got out of bed this morning. His bedroom was much like most other bedrooms. It had a four-poster bed for himself and Mrs Saurus, a rather large four-poster bed but then it would have to be a rather large bed for two Tyrannosaurus Rex to sleep in. The bed was decorated all over with intricate Christmas-themed carvings like trees, presents, stockings, candy canes and more. There were two large wooden wardrobes, and two chests of drawers with lamps on. The Santasaurus' bedside lamp was in the shape of a Nutcracker dressed in a Soldier's uniform and festive attire and Mrs. Saurus' lamp was in the shape of a Snowman which had a big orange carrot for a nose.

There was an exceptionally large mirror on the wall with a wooden frame decorated with Holly and Ivy complete with little red berries. He was excited this morning when he jumped from his bed ready to start the day. The first thing he did when he got out of bed was go to the bathroom to wash and brush his teeth.

He then got himself dressed. Being Christmas Eve there was only one thing for him to wear, his Santasaurus Suit. His Santasaurus suit is a huge red onesie with five hefty black buttons down the front the size of cookies with a big red hood that was outlined with soft fluffy white fur. The cuffs on each sleeve had fur around them too as did the bottom of each leg. Along with his suit, he wears white gloves and shiny black boots. His Santasaurus suit is incredibly special, it's what makes him who he is and it's how he is recognised all over the world. Even after all the years he's been wearing it he still feels a sense of excitement when it's time to put it on. Most surprising of all is that somehow it still fits him. As he stood there in his bedroom, he thought to himself, "Well, the sleigh isn't in here and it's definitely not in the bathroom either, so I'd better keep looking."

Chapter Five

After leaving his bedroom he made his way down the hallway to the large winding staircase at the end of the hall. As he walked down the stairs he admired the pictures he passed hanging on the wall of all the Santasaurus' that came before him going back through time over many years.

Once he reached the bottom of the stairs, he made his way to the kitchen where that morning he had sat down at the table for breakfast with Mrs Saurus as he does most mornings. Mrs Saurus had made him some jam on toast which she had lovingly cut into the shape of a Christmas tree, he had also eaten all the offcuts, "I can't see them go to waste" he had said to her. He had asked her for some mince pies for his breakfast, but she said "No, you eat too many mince pies." "You can never eat too many mince pies," he thought. To go with his Christmas tree-shaped jam on toast he had a piping hot cup of coffee (gingerbread flavoured of course). He drank it from his favourite mug which was shaped like a Christmas pudding. He stood there in the now-empty kitchen and looked around, "Nope, the sleigh isn't in here either," he said to himself, "So I'd better keep looking, but first I think I'll have another cup of coffee and maybe a mince pie... or two." As he sat once again at the kitchen table in his favourite chair drinking his coffee (this time it was Cinnamon flavoured) and eating two more of Mrs Saurus' delicious icing-topped homemade mince pies, he thought about where the sleigh could be. "I've checked the bedroom, the bathroom and now the kitchen," he thought. "Where could it be?." He was starting to worry; the day was getting on and he had a lot to do to get ready for the busy night ahead. He suddenly had a thought, "I know where it could be!" he said excitedly, jumping out of his chair and spilling crumbs all over the nice clean floor.

"The shed!, why didn't I check there first?." So, he made his way out of the kitchen, but not before he stuffed one more mince pie into his pocket for later. "You never know when you might need one", he thought.

Chapter Six

Next, he made his way to the shed. This is where his sleigh was normally stored throughout the year when it wasn't being used. The sleigh's main purpose was to be flown around the world on Christmas Eve to get the Santasaurus and the presents to where they needed to be. Sometimes though, he would take it for a flight to "blow the cobwebs off" as he put it. "I can't have my sleigh just sit in the shed all year collecting dust" he would say to Mrs Saurus. She would just nod along and smile. The shed is also where the huge green present sack was stored along with the golden yellow rope that was used to secure it closed. The sleigh was enormous and painted in the shiniest reddest paint you have ever seen. It has golden trim all around the edges from the front to the back and from the top to the bottom which glistened and sparkled in the moonlight. There were two pairs of shiny brass jingle bells at the rear on both sides and at the front of the sleigh was a large bright light to help him see what was ahead of him as he flew around the world. The most important part of the sleigh is the hot chocolate machine and the mince pie warmer to help him stay nice and cosy on a freezing cold Christmas Eve.

He stood looking around the rickety old shed when something occurred to him, it wasn't that the hole in the roof needed fixing or that the window didn't close properly anymore meaning that there was a constant chilly draft, it was that it was empty. Completely empty. No big shiny red sleigh with gold trim and brass jingle bells and no huge green present sack with a golden yellow rope that it used to secure it closed. This was not good, "I was sure that it would be in here" he said to himself. "Where have I left that sleigh!?" he asked himself once again more frustratedly than the last time.

He trudged out of the shed and into the bright light of the day feeling slightly deflated. As he stepped outside he was suddenly aware of the ice-cold air of the North Pole as it hit him and made the tip of his nose tingle. "Now what?" he thought.

Chapter Seven

The Santasaurus sat on the ground under a huge evergreen spruce tree with soft green and yellow-tipped twigs. In the process of sitting down he disturbed some of the slender branches and ended up covered in a layer of snow himself. He was beginning to think that he wouldn't find the sleigh in time for the Christmas Eve flight or even find it at all. He couldn't help but think about all the children waking up on Christmas morning and looking under their Christmas trees to discover that there were no presents. "What would they do?, What would they think?" he whispered to himself over and over again. "I just cannot let this happen!." "All of those children, they can't go without presents." "Where could it be?, I've looked everywhere" he exclaimed.

He started running the day's events back through his mind. "Firstly, I looked in my bedroom and the bathroom, but it wasn't there, then I made my way to the kitchen, but it wasn't there either, although I did find some more mince pies." He was pleased about the mince pies, but they didn't make him feel better about the Sleigh situation. After the kitchen, he had looked in the shed. "I was positive that the sleigh was going to be in the shed, it's always in the shed" He sat a while longer in his spot under the tree still feeling a little gloomy and had a think about where he could go and look next. "Where next?, where can I look?"

Within a moment an idea came to him, an idea so simple that he was annoyed that it hadn't presented itself before now. "I'll go to the Workshop!" he thought to himself. He thought that it must be there or at least that someone in the Workshop might have seen it. He always liked going to the Workshops and seeing the Elves. They were a jovial bunch, and they never failed to make the

Santasaurus smile with glee when he was around them.

He stood up from his spot on the frozen ground, gave himself a shake to offload some of the snow and marched off in the direction of the Workshop.

Chapter Eight

As he arrived at the front of the Workshop he stopped and looked at the enormous oak arched double doors that stood front and centre. There was a rather bulky cast iron door knocker shaped like a pinecone on the door on the right that was painted black. These days no one used the knocker as there was now a very clever wireless doorbell and camera system in place that played any tune you wanted, as long as it was a Christmas one. It currently played the tune of 'Jingle Bells.' The tune changed now and again, it was always chosen by one of the Elves as a birthday treat.

The workshop is the beating heart of the village and it's also home to the Santasaurus' helpers, the Elves. This is where they live, work and sleep. They are Compsognathus dinosaurs or Compi's as they are better known (mostly because no one can pronounce their proper name). Compi Elves are very hardworking, they are small, agile, and work well as a team. There are hundreds of these tiny dinosaurs busy at work mending and making, building, and crafting. The Workshop is always filled with the sound of hammers pounding, saws whirring, paint splashing and moving parts squeaking. The Santasaurus' most trusted Elf is called Pickme. Pickme got his name because whenever the Santasaurus asked for help, Pickme would be the first to put his hand in the air, jump up and down and shout, 'Pick me!, pick me!.' Pickme is the Chief Elf, which means that he oversees the workshop and the whole toy production line from design, to building to when they're finally boxed and ready to go. He is also in charge of all the other Elves, and he makes sure they are working hard but also that they are having fun because that's what being an Elf is all about. Part of this fun is that they like to sing songs as they work, and their favourite song to sing is…

"We make toys for the girls and boys,

We make them in our special way,

*

Some are quiet and some make noise,

Then Santa delivers them on his sleigh,

*

We make toys for the girls and boys,

So, they can have fun on Christmas Day."

The workshop is not only where all the toys are made but also where the sleigh has its maintenance done when it needs an upgrade or is repaired when it gets damaged. It had recently been in for an upgrade and is now fitted with a state-of-the-art electronic moving map system to help the Santasaurus accurately and precisely navigate around the world, the SUPER ACCURATE NAVIGATIONAL TALKING ASSISTANT, or 'S.A.N.T.A NAV' as it was known for short.

As he stood looking around the workshop at the Elves hard at work, he heard someone shouting, 'Santa, Santa!.' He turned to see Pickme running towards him. All Compi Elves are known to be short at only two to three feet tall, but Pickme was particularly so, if not maybe a little shorter than most. Pickme was wearing what he and the other Elves always wore, a fluffy pointy hat (Pickme's was green) with a bell at its tip and light brown fur around the base, a waistcoat made up of reds, greens and browns of all shades in a kind of patchwork manner. As Chief Elf, Pickme also wore a bronze medallion which hung around his neck on a yellow ribbon which was embossed with a picture of three stacked gift-wrapped boxes with ribbons tied in bows on them. After what felt like a long time, Pickme finally made it to where the Santasaurus was standing. "Santa, what brings you here?" asked Pickme, "I wanted to see how you were all getting on" replied Santa, trying not to sound too panicked about the real reason for his visit. "How is everything going here? Are you all ready for tonight?" asked Santa casually. "Yes, everything is on schedule." "The last of the presents are being wrapped now, then that's all one billion, nine hundred and forty-seven million, three hundred and sixty-two thousand, five hundred and eighteen presents finished." Said Pickme proudly. "Wow, I think I'm going to need a bigger sack" says the Santasaurus, "Especially if I can't find the one I'm supposed to have" he mumbled under his breath so Pickme couldn't hear. "Whilst we're on the subject of the present sack, have you seen it….. and the sleigh?" asked Santa. "No, I haven't" said Pickme, "We've all been working hard over the past few days making the finishing touches to the presents and getting them ready for Christmas. The last time I saw the sleigh was when it was in here having the S.A.N.T.A NAV installed a few days ago."

"Um," thought Santa, "So the sleigh definitely was in here but now it's not, so where could it be?"

He left Pickme and the other Compi Elves to finish getting everything ready as he went outside to try and find his sleigh. "Goodbye," said Santa with a wave of his hand on his way out. "Goodbye Santa, thanks for dropping by" shouted Pickme.

Chapter Nine

Finally, he decided to look in the barn. The barn is a great wooden structure with stables inside, it has two huge sliding doors at the front which open to a large open space with box stalls going down both sides. There are a mixture of small individual stalls and some much larger ones. The large stable near the entrance to the barn is where one of the most important parts of the whole sleigh is kept, this is what powers the sleigh so that it can fly to every home around the world in just one night. These are Velociraptors, eight Velociraptors to be precise, and together they pull the Santasaurus' sleigh.

The Santasaurus slowly and guardedly slid open one of the doors and looked inside the barn to see if his sleigh was there. He peered into the dark but couldn't see anything so he decided to creep in as quietly as he could. He didn't want to disturb the Velociraptors because although they are strong, fast and powerful which makes them the perfect dinosaurs for pulling the sleigh, they can also be a bit excitable, especially if they're hungry. As he crept in he could see that they were busy eating, so they weren't interested in what he was doing anyway. It was pitch black in the barn, so he started feeling around for the big metal lever to turn the lights on, he found the lever and pulled it down. One after another the huge bright lights of the barn began to come on with a boom one row at a time, working their way from the front to the back of the room,

BOOM!...BOOM!...BOOM!

As the lights warmed up and got brighter, he could make out something twinkling and glistening at the far end of the barn.

"IT'S MY SLEIGH... AND THE PRESENTS!"

he shouted excitedly, pleased that he had finally found it. He shouted it a lot louder than he meant to, startling both the raptors and himself in the process. The Raptors stopped eating for a moment and looked in his direction, but after a few moments they decided that their food was more interesting and went back to filling their bellies. "Thank goodness," said the Santasaurus, "I was beginning to lose all hope of ever finding it." He rushed to the sleigh which was located at the back of the stable with the towering green sack of presents sitting on top of it with its golden yellow rope tied in a decorative and secure bow.

Chapter Ten

As he approached the sleigh he could hear a noise, it was coming from the rear of the barn. He took a few steps closer to see if he could see what it was, he could hear that the noise was coming from the large wooden door at the rear of the barn. The hefty wooden door was opening slowly, and its rusty old hinges were making a loud creaking sound.

CREEAAK!!!

He could see the shadow of someone appearing from behind the door as they started to make their way in, the door opening wider while the hinges continued to groan. The last row of lights was still dim so he couldn't make out who the shadowy figure was that was now approaching him. As the lights finally warmed up and got brighter he realised that it was Mrs Saurus. "Hello Dear," she said. "Hello," he said in return, relieved and trying not to look at all scared, "What are you doing in the barn?" he asked. "I've been here all day. I've been helping the Elves with their final checks and making sure that you have everything you need for your journey tonight." "Well," he began, "I've spent all day looking for my sleigh and the presents as I couldn't find them anywhere. I thought I'd never find them." "Sounds like you've had a very busy day" said Mrs Saurus, "but…" she continued, "I did tell you this morning that the sleigh had been moved out of the shed and into the barn and that it was being prepared for the journey ahead," "Well, I don't remember that," he said, more to himself than to Mrs Saurus as he stood scratching his head and feeling a little confused. "That Dear," said Mrs Saurus with a smile on her face, "is because you don't listen." The Santasaurus stood there knowing that this was often true. He also knew that without Mrs Saurus' help, nothing would ever get done.

"How have the preparations been going," he asked, trying to quickly change the subject. "Very well" she replied, "The Elves and I have been awfully busy putting the finishing touches to the sleigh, collecting together the harnesses and feeding the Raptors so they have enough energy for their flight." "Well, it sounds like you have been very busy indeed" he said, "Now that I'm here I think that I should help, I will start by doing my pre-flight checks."

Chapter Eleven

The Santasaurus was feeling a lot jollier and more festive now that he had finally found his sleigh and the presents. He began to walk around the sleigh checking that everything was in order. He checked that the light at the front worked and that it would be bright enough to show the way and he checked the jingle bells to make sure that they still made their magical jingling sound. The sleigh was facing the front of the barn and had two sets of reins laid out in front. The two sets of reins were made of shiny black patent leather, and each of the two reins had four harnesses made from the same leather, these were used to secure the Raptors to the sleight. Each of the harnesses had two more shiny brass jingle bells matching those on the sleigh.

The sleigh was shinier than he had ever seen it, its smooth red paint and gold trim glistening under the lights of the barn. It sat with the bulging sack of presents carefully balanced on the back. This was always a remarkable sight. He wasn't sure how the Compi Elves managed to get all those presents in the sack and secure it close it, but somehow they always do. They would then carefully carry the sack and balance it safely on the back of the sleigh. It is then secured in place so that it doesn't fall off during the flight. Along with the presents, his trusty Raptors were secured in place in their harnesses ready to fly off into the night. The Raptors were getting restless, their excitement was unmistakable as they waited to be harnessed, they just nuzzled each other and pawed at the ground, eager to take to the skies. The Santasaurus stood back and took a good look, he said nothing, just smiled and nodded to himself.

Chapter Twelve

At last, the Santasaurus was ready for Christmas Eve. The presents were loaded, and the Raptors were harnessed ready to take flight and soar through the crisp winter air, delivering presents with Santa to children all over the world. It was a magical sight to behold, and everyone who witnessed it couldn't help but feel a sense of wonder and joy. He put his hand in his pocket and pulled out his list. "Better do one last check", he thought.

He looked at the crumpled piece of paper,

- Santa Suit
- Sleigh
- Sack full of presents
- Present list (make sure you check it twice!)
- ~~MORE MINCE PIES~~

This time he was happy that he had everything, well except for the extra mince pies, suddenly he remembered the one that he had stuffed into his pocket as he left the kitchen, "You never know when you might need one", he thought to himself again with a little chuckle.

"All set, Dear?" asked Mrs Saurus. "Almost," he said, faffing about, trying to sort something out in the sleigh just out of sight, "I just have one final thing that I need to do before I can get on my way", he said, "Which is to turn on the hot chocolate machine and set the timer on the mince pie warmer." He leaned forward against his harness which was feeling a little tighter than he remembered from last year, "Must be new harnesses" he thought, "Yes that'll be it". He stretched out his gloved finger to press one of the buttons on the mince pie warmer but noticed that it was already on. He sat back up in his seat and looked at Mrs Saurus who looked back at him smiling with a nod, "Thank you" he said. She had already gotten everything ready for him. The sleigh was then led out of the Barn by two of the Elves who held onto the harness at the front.

The air was crisp and cold, and the snow on the ground crunched beneath their feet. The Raptors each pawed at the ground and snorted as their feet touched the cold snow. The sleigh was lined up ready for it to take flight. Mrs Saurus and the Elves stood clear as the sleigh began to slowly move forward under the steam of the Raptors. It got faster and faster and finally, the Santasaurus pulled back hard on the reins and the Raptors, and the sleigh left the ground and took flight. The Santasaurus looked back and gave a wave and a faint "Ho! Ho! Ho!" Which could hardly be heard over the circulating wind and the sound of the Elves cheering.

"As he sprang to his sleigh with his Raptors in sight, he was heard to exclaim before they started their flight."

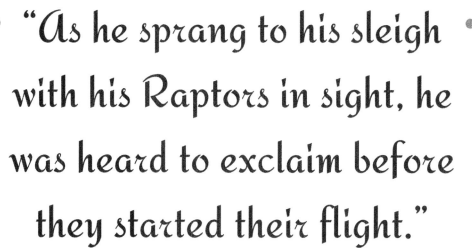

"Happy Christmas to all, and to all a good night."

OTHER TITLES

"DINOBORE is a roarin' good time!

Join this charming dinosaur on an adventure filled with fun, friendship, and a lesson that being unique isn't boring at all!"

"Tessa's the Triceratops has a Dream".

"Follow the heartwarming journey of a little Triceratops with a big dream: to become a mermaid. Join her as she explores her longing for the sea, friendship, and the love of home."

 @Matthew_WritesBooks

Printed in Great Britain
by Amazon